SERMON OUTLINES

on

The Book of Psalms

Also by Al Bryant

SERMON OUTLINES

on

The Book of Psalms

compiled by
Al Bryant

PUBLICATIONS

Grand Rapids, MI 49501

Sermon Outlines on the Book of Psalms
compiled by Al Bryant

© 1997 by Kregel Publications, a division of Kregel, Inc.,
P.O. Box 2607, Grand Rapids, MI 49501.

All rights reserved. No part of this book may be repro-
duced, stored in a retrieval system, or transmitted in any
form or by any means—electronic, mechanical, photo-
copy, recording, or otherwise—without written permission of the publisher, except for brief quotations in printed
reviews.

For more information about Kregel Publications, visit our
web site at: www.kregel.com

Library of Congress Cataloging-in-Publication
Sermon outlines on the book of Psalms / compiled by Al
Bryant.
     p.   cm.
1. Bible. O.T. Psalms—Sermons—Outlines, syllabi, etc. I.
Bryant, Al.
BS1430.4.S47   1997   251'.02—dc21   97-30133

ISBN 0-8254-2066-0

2 3 4 5 6 printing / year 04 03 02 01 00

Printed in the United States of America

CONTENTS

PREFACE

One of the most loved books of the Bible is the Psalms. This collection of sermon outlines represents only a small segment of the many possibilities for preaching through the Psalms available to the seeker of truth in this blessed book.

Whatever the believer's need, he or she will find it addressed somewhere in this collection. The Psalms were penned by sometimes beleaguered believers, and they deal with the real problems of their lives. These "songs" also reflect the joyful praise of one who found God faithful in the midst of trials and tribulations. Indeed, the Hebrew name for this book meant "The Book of Praises." I hope you will find this selection of sermon outlines both useful and uplifting.

AL BRYANT

*The poems in this compilation are used by permission and taken from *Sourcebook of Poetry,* published in 1992 by Kregel Publications.

SCRIPTURE INDEX

LIKE A TREE

He shall be like a tree (Ps. 1:3).

Man is usually likened to changing grass, fading flowers, chaff (v. 4). But a tree is:

1. **A Fixed Thing.**
   Roots deep—"planted by rivers." Trees do not plant themselves. God-planted—"trees of the Lord."

2. **A Growing Thing.**
   "By the rivers of water." Nutriment; best position.

3. **A Living Thing.**
   During winter and summer keeps on developing—"leaf also shall not wither." God-imparted life.

4. **A Beautiful Thing.**
   "Like a tree." Few objects in nature are so pleasing as a prosperous tree.

Selected

Trees

In every path of timber you
Will always find a tree or two
That would have fallen long ago,
Borne down by wind or age or snow,
Had not another neighbor tree
Held out its arms in sympathy
And caught the tree that the storm had hurled
To earth. So, neighbors, is the world.
In every patch of timber stand
Samaritans of forest land,
The birch, the maple, oak, and pine,
The fir, the cedar, all in line!

In every wood unseen, unknown,
They bear their burdens of their own
And bear as well another form,
Some neighbor stricken in the storm.
Shall trees be nobler to their kind
Than men, who boast the noble mind;
Shall there exist within the wood
This great eternal brotherhood
Of oak and pine, of hill and fen,
And not within the hearts of men?
God grant that men are like to these,
And brothers, brotherly as trees.

—Author Unknown

GETTING RID OF TWIST

You give blessings to the pure, but pains to those who leave your paths
(Ps. 18:26 LB).

One translator or version used the word *twisted* to convey the idea of departure from God's paths.

1. One's Idea of God Is According to One's Own "Twist."

When my attitude and action are twisted as regards the brotherhood of man, it is safe to say that I have a twisted idea of the Fatherhood of God. Can the unforgiving man plumb the deep wonder of the forgiveness of God? Can a man who hates his brother know the love of God? Can the hard man know the tender mercy of God? Can the proud man understand the humility of Jesus?

2. Twist Persists.

Who has not noticed the persistence of a twist or the tendency to twist in a fabric or cord? So it is with our human natures. And that is perhaps one reason why our sanctification or growth in grace is so slow. It takes time to get rid of the twist.

3. But Christ Is Very Patient.

The good work He began with us will be completed. There is great joy in the new and larger vision of God that comes as one's perversity passes. "With the pure thou wilt show thyself pure." "Blessed are the pure in heart [the untwisted?]: for they shall see God" (Matt. 5:8).

M. K. V. Heicher

OUR HEAVENLY FATHER has a definite plan for our lives. God does not merely make souls and send them out into this world to take bodies and grow up amid crowds of other souls with bodies, to take their chances and make what they can of their destinies. He plans specifically for each of our lives. He deals with us as individuals. He knows us by name, and loves us each one with a love as distinct and personal as if each was the only child He had on this earth. His plan for each life is always a beautiful plan, too, for He never designs marring and ruin for a life. He never made a human soul for the express purpose of being lost. God's design for each life is that it shall reach a holy character, do a good work in the world, fill a worthy place, however humble, and fill it well, so as to honor God and bless the world.

—Al Bryant

But let all those that put their trust in thee rejoice:
let them ever shout for joy, because thou defendest them:
let them also that love thy name be joyful in thee (Ps. 5:11).

Rejoice evermore (1 Thess. 5:16).

The grace of God can make us sing when suffering (Acts 16:25), rejoice when persecuted (Acts 5:41), bless when cursed (Matt. 5:44), content when buffeted (2 Cor. 12:7–9), merry when saved (Luke 15:24), joyful when tried (2 Cor. 7:4), and lifted up when cast down (2 Cor. 4:9–11).

Payson, in his last days, said: "Christians might avoid much trouble and inconvenience if they would only believe what they profess, that God is able to make them happy without anything else. They imagine that if such a dear friend were to die, or such-and-such blessings were to be removed, they would be miserable. Whereas God can make them a thousand times happier without them. To mention my own case: God has been depriving me of one blessing after another, but as every one was removed He has come in and filled up its place. Now when I am a cripple and not able to move, I am happier than I ever was in my life before, or ever expected to be. If I had believed this twenty years ago, I might have been spared much anxiety."

Determination in exultation is a sign of grace. If we practice well, we shall sing harmoniously.

1. **The One We Praise**—"I will praise thee, O [Jehovah]" (Ps. 9:1). He is the faithful and unchanging One. We can rest in the solidarity of His love and rely on the sovereignty of His grace.

2. **The Reason of Our Song**—"I will sing unto [Jehovah], because he hath dealt bountifully with me" (Ps. 13:6). His bounties are lasting love, living grace, and lifting power. We have something about which we can sing.

3. **The Power of Which We Chant**—"I will sing of thy power" (Ps. 59:16). He gives power to be, to do, to suffer, to witness, to fight, and to rest in Himself. He never calls us to do anything without qualifying us for it.

4. **The Mercies Which Come**—"I will sing of the mercies of the LORD" (Ps. 89:1). His mercies are continuous in their blessing, faithful in their service, loving in their kindness, holy in their ministry, and suitable in their application.

5. **The Heart Which Sings**—"O God, my heart is fixed; I will sing and give praise" (Ps. 108:1). The heart which is tuned to praise is the heart that is fixed on the Lord and is content with the Lord.

6. **The Instrument with Which We Sing**—"I will sing a new song unto thee, O God: upon a psaltery and an instrument of ten strings will I sing praises unto thee" (Ps. 144:9). The ten strings of our body should praise Him— our eyes by looking to Him, our ears by their attention, our hands by our work, our feet by our walk, our tongue by our speech, and our heart by our love.

7. **Where We Sing**—"I will sing unto thee among the nations" (Ps. 57:9). We praise Him truthfully and triumphantly when we live for Him wholly.

F. E. Marsh

"THE LORD . . . is my *song,*" says Isaiah (12:2). That is to say, the Lord is the giver of our songs. He breathes the music into the hearts of His people; He is the Creator of their joy. The Lord is also the subject of their songs. They sing of Him and of all that He does on their behalf. The Lord is, moreover, the object of their song; they sing to the Lord. Their praise is meant for Him alone. They do not make melody for human ears, but to the Lord. "The LORD . . . is my song." Then I ought always to sing. And if I sing my loudest, I can never reach the height of this great argument, nor come to the end of it. This song never changes. If I live by faith my song is always the same, for "the LORD . . . is my song." Our song to God is God Himself. He alone can express our intensest joy. O God, You are my exceeding joy. Father, Son, and Holy Spirit, You are my hymn of everlasting delight.

—Spurgeon

WHAT IS MAN?

Psalm 8:4

I. He Is a Child of the Dust.
A. Human, earthly, mortal.
B. Created so.

II. He Is a Child of God.
A. The thought of God (Gen. 1:26).
B. The creation of God (Gen. 1:27).
C. The image and likeness of God (Gen. 1:27). This image is mental, not moral. It was not lost in the fall. It consists of mind, intelligence, sensibility, and will. If it had been lost in the fall, the Bible would have mentioned it (see Gen. 5:1; 9:6; 1 Cor. 11:7; James 3:9).

III. Man Is an Object of God's Love and Care.
God loves him, is mindful of him, visits him, protects him, and provides for him.

IV. Man Is the Subject of Wonderful Achievement.

V. Man Is the Subject of Wonderful Possibilities.
A. Socially, intellectually, and morally.
B. Created like God mentally, he can, he may, become like God morally. Like God mentally by creation. Like God morally by recreation or regeneration.

Selected

God, Thou Hast Made the World Beautiful

God—Thou hast made the world so beautiful!
A flock of birds on pinions fleet and strong,
Then—though it were not yet enough to soar—
    Gave to them song.
God—Thou hast made the world so beautiful;
A bower of June roses gay abloom,
Then—though it were not yet enough to grow—
    Gave them perfume.
God—Thou hast made the world so beautiful;
A million beings, soul their priceless gem,
Then—though it were not yet enough to live—
    Gave love to them.

—Theodosia Pearce

GOOD CHEER FOR THE NEEDY

For the needy shall not always be forgotten:
the expectation of the poor shall not perish for ever (Ps. 9:18).

The practical value of a text very much depends upon the man to whom it comes. The song of the troubadour was charming to Richard Coeur de Lion because he knew the responsive verses. The trail is full of meaning to the Indian, for his quick eye knows how to follow it; it would not mean as much to a white settler. The sight of the lighthouse is cheering to the mariner, for from it he gathers his whereabouts. So will those who are spiritually poor and needy eagerly lay hold on this promise, prize it, and live upon it with contentment.

I. Two Bitter Experiences Ended.

A. "The needy shall not always be forgotten." You have been forgotten:

- By former friends and admirers.
- In arrangements made and plans projected.
- In judgments formed and in praises distributed.
- In help estimated and reliance expressed.

In fact, you have not been a factor in the calculation; you have been forgotten as a dead man out of mind. This has wounded you deeply, for there was a time when you were consulted among the first. This will not so always be.

B. "The expectation of the poor shall not perish forever." You have been disappointed:

- In your natural expectation from justice, gratitude, relationship, age, sympathy, charity, etc.
- In your confidence in man.
- In your judgment of yourself.
- In your expectations of providence.

This disappointment shall only be temporary. Your expectation shall not perish forever; you shall yet receive more than you expected.

II. Two Sad Fears Removed. Fears which are naturally suggested by what you have already experienced.

A. Not forever shall you be forgotten:

- You shall not meet with final forgetfulness.
- In the day of severe trouble.

- In the night of grief and alarm for sin.
- In the hour of death.

B. Nor shall your expectation perish:
- Your weakness shall not frustrate the power of God.
- Your sin shall not dry up the grace of God.
- Your constitutional infirmities shall not cause your overthrow.

Your future trials shall not be too much for you.

III. Two Sweet Promises Given.

A. "Not always be forgotten"; you shall not be overlooked:
- At the mercy seat, when you are pleading.
- From the pulpit, and in the Word, when your soul is hungering.
- In your sufferings and service, when to be thought of by the Lord will be your main consolation.

B. "Expectation shall not perish for ever." You shall not be disappointed:
- Peace shall visit your heart.
- Sin shall be vanquished without and within.
- Let the poor man hope in God.
- Let him feast on the future if he find the present to be scant.
- Above all, let him rest in the promise of a faithful God.

An aged Christian lying on his deathbed in a state of such extreme weakness that he was often entirely unconscious of all around him, was asked the cause of his perfect peace. He replied, "When I am able to think, I think of Jesus; and when I am unable to think of Him, I know He is thinking of me."

THIRTY YEARS AGO before the Lord caused me to wander from my father's house and from my native place, I put my mark upon this passage in Isaiah: "Thou shalt know that I am the LORD," etc. (49:23). Of the many books I now possess, the Bible that bears this mark is the only one that belonged to me at that time. It now lies before me, and I find that, although the hair which then was dark as night has meanwhile become silvered, the ink which marked this text has darkened as the time advanced, corresponding with, and in fact recording, the growing intensity of the conviction that "they shall not be ashamed that wait for me." I *believed*

15

it then, but I *know* it now, and I can write *"Probatum est"* with my whole heart over against the symbol which that mark is to me of my ancient faith. . . . Under many perilous circumstances, in many most trying scenes, amid faintings within and fears without, and under tortures that rend the heart and troubles that crush it down, I have waited for You, and lo! I stand this day as one not ashamed.
                                                                    —*John Kitto*

                                                                    Spurgeon

---

HOW NATURE PREACHES

*The heavens declare the glory of God;
and the firmament showeth his handiwork (Ps. 19:1).*

Nature exists not for a merely natural but for a moral end; not alone for what it is, but for what it says or declares. God looks upon nature as a basis of language. The heavenly objects are signs. Signs are vehicles of ideas. They say something. The universe is God's telephone system, His grand signal system by which He flashes messages from the heights above to the deepest valleys below. The material system is God's great instrument of conversation. "The heavens declare the glory of God; and the firmament showeth his handiwork."

1. The Fact of Nature Reveals the Being of God.

2. The Vastness of Nature Shows His Immensity.

3. The Uniformity of Nature Declares His Unity.

4. The Regularity of Nature Discloses His Unchangeableness.

5. The Variety of Nature Manifests His Exhaustlessness.

6. The Adaptations of Nature Unveil His Wisdom.

7. The Happiness of Nature Displays His Goodness.

Nature tells us to think of God. God would have us contemplate nature. It is not His only revelation, but it is a very great and beautiful one. God's testimony is of both the works and the Word. Nature is a volume in which the Godhead of the Creator is plainly discoverable. Scripture is the volume in which all may read the Divine will concerning them. Study both.

                                                                    Hallock

---

"MY GOD"

O my God, I trust in thee (Ps. 25:2).

See the words "my God" as to what relationship with Him means in the following Scriptures:

1. All **supplied** (Phil. 4:19).

2. All **enemies** defeated (Ps. 7:1).

3. All **safety** found (Ps. 18:2).

4. All **light** given (Ps. 18:28).

5. All **healing** bestowed (Ps. 30:2).

6. All **worship** rendered (Ps. 43:4).

7. All **thirst** satisfied (Ps. 63:1).

F. E. Marsh

DIVINE SECRETS IN PSALM 16

1. Secret of a **Life of Trust**—I trust in Him (v. 1).

2. Secret of a **Surrendered Life**—I belong to Him (v. 2).

3. Secret of a **Separated Life**—I side with Him (vv. 3–4).

4. Secret of a **Happy Life**—I am satisfied with Him (vv. 5–6).

5. Secret of an **Instructed Life**—I listen to Him (v. 7).

6. Secret of a **Steadfast Life**—I am engaged with Him (v. 8ff.).

Pickering

TWO VITAL PRAYERS

Lead me in thy truth, and teach me:
for thou art the God of my salvation;
on thee do I wait all the day (Ps. 25:5).

Here are indeed two vital prayers with a reason or argument attached.

1. Consider First the Prevalent Pleader—the Psalmist.

He prays, "Lead me." His character is shown by his prayer. There is humility. "Lead me." I feel that I cannot walk alone.

"Teach me." I realize my ignorance. In this he shows his wisdom for he prays for the best things and uses the chiefest argument. His faith.

"I wait." Evidently expecting an answer. His patience. He had waited long, but is willing to tarry for God's time. He prays and waits; thus God is honored. He waits and prays; thus his earnestness and anxiety are shown.

2. The Twofold Prayer.

"Lead me . . . teach me." "Lead me," that is, help me to walk according to your will. "Teach me," that is, even though your leading may be contrary to my expectations. For joy I may have bitterness; for a wealthy place I may have a desert.

3. The Manifold Argument.

"For thou art the God of my salvation." How well the psalmist has ordered his plea; for God has engaged to keep His own. "I will never leave thee nor forsake thee." And Jesus has promised to teach us. In the after days He said He would send His Spirit to lead us into all truth. He also revealed His desire that the redeemed should recognize and celebrate His faithfulness. He who could put our feet in the right path will surely guide our steps therein. "Lead me." "Teach me."

Selected

FEATURES OF A WHOLEHEARTED CHRISTIAN

Psalm 26

1. He desires to be tested by God (vv. 1–2).

2. He has faith in God (v. 1).

3. He adheres to the Word of God (v. 3).

4. He separates Himself from the enemies of God (v. 4).

5. He offers sacrifice to God (v. 6).

6. He testifies for God (v. 7).

7. He loves the House of God (v. 8 RV).

8. He praises the Name of God (v. 12).

WAIT BEFORE YOU GO

Wait on the LORD: be of good courage, and he shall strengthen thine heart: wait, I say, on the LORD (Ps. 27:14).

The little word *wait* is small but potent. As it is used here it has three distinct meanings.

1. ***Wait* Means Pray.**

Pray in the sense of quietness and meditation: Be quiet before God, commune with Him. "I don't want anything," said the little girl as she came into her father's study. "I just want to be near you and be quiet."

2. ***Wait* Means Work.**

We are to work as well as wait. "There is no use saying our prayers unless our prayers mean guidance for service," said Robert Norwood.

3. ***Wait* Means Tarry.**

Do not hurry God. Do not be impatient with Him. Thirty-eight years the impotent man waited at the pool—and not in vain. "In your patience ye shall win your souls."

Bruce S. Wright

TURBULENT TIMES AND GOD'S REIGN

The LORD sitteth upon the flood; yea, the LORD sitteth King forever (Ps. 29:10).

This is a comforting text for a troubled time.

I. **It reveals, first, a turbulent scene.**
"Flood."

A. A flood suggests commotion. In the moral domain. Spiritually. Nationally. Internationally.

B. A flood suggests innovation. Breaking down of barriers.

C. A flood suggests distress. Furious and violent. The moral world is not like a river flowing on peacefully in its channel. It is "flood."

II. **It reveals, second, a tranquil God.**
"The LORD sitteth." This implies on His part:

A. Consciousness of His right to reign. If He had any moral misgivings He would not be at ease. A usurper could not be tranquil over such a tumultuous empire.

B. A consciousness of supremacy of power to reign. No feeling of incapacity. God can control with consummate ease the whole. Rejoice.

Selected

The Lord Jehovah Reigns

The Lord Jehovah reigns,
His throne is built on high;
The garments He assumes
Are light and majesty;
His glories shine with beams so bright,
No mortal eye can bear the sight. . . .

And will this sovereign King
Of glory condescend,
And will He write His name,
My Father and my Friend?
I love His name, I love His Word;
Join all my powers to praise the Lord!

—Isaac Watts

MY CHURCH AND MY COUNTRY
(HOME MISSIONS)

Blessed is the nation whose God is the LORD (Ps. 33:12).

Here is a promise with a condition. The condition, "Whose God is the Lord." Not tribal or national gods. Not gods of science, efficiency, power, wealth, success. But the God and Father of us all.

1. Who Is to Be Worshiped.

All idols are to be removed from the national shrine! No other gods can come before Him. His courts can be entered with thanksgiving and His gates with praise.

2. Who Is to Be Obeyed.

In His service the nation can say, "I delight to do thy will." He embodies His law in the law of the land. He seeks to make the fundamental principles of Jesus the principles of the commonwealth.

3. Who Is to Be Honored with Substance.

Institutions dedicated to His name and for the extension of His kingdom are to be supported. He is to be honored with at least as much support as a chewing gum manufacturer, as much money spent on Christian education as on movies and as much for missions as for food and cosmetics.

4. The Promise: "Blessed Is That Nation."

A. In its civic and political life: With citizenship held as a trust from God, intelligent, loyal, and more concerned about duties than rights. Choosing leaders to administer office for the glory of God and for the national welfare, promoting the liberty wherewith Christ has made us free.

B. In its industrial life: Free from extremes of poverty and wealth; no "forgotten men." Freedom from racial prejudice, class hatred, etc. Opportunities to develop every talent to the fullest capacity.

We will never solve our national problems until God is indeed the Lord; until the motto, "In God we trust," on our coinage is translated into a motive in our national career.

Selected

SALVATION

Blessed is he whose transgression is forgiven, whose sin is covered (Ps. 32:1).

Introduction
- A. Salvation and religion are two different things.
- B. Salvation is vitally necessary to inherit eternal life.
- C. Salvation is of God (3:8; 37:39).

I. Salvation Begins with Revelation (27:1; 31:5).
- A. See God—see yourself reflected (85:9).
- B. See yourself—see your need (34:18).
- C. See your need—seek a Savior (31:5).

II. Salvation Is Given the Desperate Seeker (39:8).
- A. Must want salvation through deliverance (69:14).
- B. Genuine desire for godly fruition (69:18).
- C. Not, "If God wants to," but, "God must do it for me."

III. Salvation Is Contingent upon Meeting Conditions.
- A. God's moral standard (7:10).
- B. Carrying out God's commandments (119:166).
- C. Delighting in God's law (119:174).

Conclusion

Salvation brings enjoyment of the blessings of God (51:12). "Let the redeemed of the LORD say so" (107:2).

Gene Mallory

GOD, WHO CANNOT LIE—God, who cannot err—tells us what it is to be blessed. Here in Psalm 32:1 He declares that "blessed is he whose transgression is forgiven, whose sin is covered." This is an oracle not to be disputed. Forgiven sin is better than accumulated wealth. The remission of sin is infinitely to be preferred before all the glitter and the glare of this world's prosperity. The gratification of creature passions and earthly desires is illusive—a shadow and a fiction. But the blessedness of the justified, the blessedness of the man to whom God imputes righteousness is substantial and true.

—Spurgeon

THE "ALL" PSALM

Psalm 34 RV

1. **A Joyful Chorister.** "I will bless [Jehovah] at *all* times" (v. 1).

2. **A Delivered Suppliant.** "[Jehovah] . . . delivered me from *all* my fears" (v. 4).

3. **A Saved Saint.** "[Jehovah] . . . saved him out of *all* his troubles" (v. 6).

4. **A Confident Witness.** "[Jehovah] heareth, and delivereth them out of *all* their troubles" (v. 17).

5. **An Escaped Believer.** "Afflictions . . . [Jehovah] delivereth him out of them *all*" (v. 19).

6. **A Preserved Servant.** "He keepeth *all* his bones" (v. 20).

F. E. Marsh

All people that on earth do dwell,
Sing to the Lord with cheerful voice;
Him serve with fear, his praise forth tell,
Come ye before him and rejoice.

The Lord, ye know, is God indeed;
Without our aid he did us make:
We are his flock, he doth us feed,
And for his sheep he doth us take.

Oh, enter, then, his gates with praise,
Approach with joy his courts unto;
Praise, laud, and bless his name always,
For it is seemly so to do.

For why? the Lord our God is good,
His mercy is forever sure;
His truth at all times firmly stood,
And shall from age to age endure.

—*William Kethe*

1. **What Man Is.**
   "Every man at his best state is altogether vanity" (Ps. 39:5).

2. **What Man Has Become.**
   "Altogether become filthy" (Ps. 53:3).

3. **What God's Word Is.**
   "The judgments of [Jehovah] are true and righteous altogether" (Ps. 19:9).

4. **What God Thinks about Man's Thinking about Himself.**
   "Thou thoughtest that I was altogether such an one as thyself" (Ps. 50:21).

5. **What the Convicted Saint Knows God Knows.**
   "There is not a word in my tongue, but, lo, O [Jehovah], thou knowest it altogether" (Ps. 139:4).

6. **God's Other Blessing of His People.**
   "Thou hast altogether blessed them these three times . . . what the Lord saith, that will I speak" (Num. 23:11, 26; 24:1, 10, 13).

7. **The Secret of Blessing.**
   "That which is altogether just shalt thou follow, that thou mayest live, and inherit the land" (Deut. 16:20).

F. E. Marsh

Be Still, My Soul

Be still, my soul: the Lord is on thy side;
Bear patiently the cross of grief or pain;
Leave to thy God to order and provide;
In every change the faithful will remain.
Be still, my soul: thy best, thy heavenly Friend
Through thorny ways leads to a joyful end.

Be still, my soul: thy God doth undertake
To guide the future as he has the past.
Thy hope, thy confidence let nothing shake;
All now mysterious shall be bright at last.
Be still, my soul: the waves and winds still know
His voice who ruled them while he dwelt below.

—Katharina von Schlegel

SALUS JEHOVAE
(SALVATION IS OF THE LORD)

But the salvation of the righteous is of the LORD (Ps. 37:39).

Salvation is a term that describes the whole life of true believers—their whole experience, from their first consciousness of the ruin of the fall to their entrance into glory. They feel their need of being perpetually saved from self, sin, Satan, and the world. They trust in God for preservation, and their end is peace (v. 37).

I. This Is the Essence of Sound Doctrine.

The salvation of the righteous is of the Lord, even of the Triune Jehovah—Father, Son, and Holy Spirit in:

A. The planning.

B. The providing.

C. The beginning.

D. The carrying on.

E. The completion.

II. This Is a Necessary Fact.

The saints recognize it, for:

A. Their inward conflicts make them know that God alone must work salvation. They are too fickle and feeble to save themselves.

B. Their outward temptations drive them to the same conclusion. They are well kept whom God keeps, but none else.

C. The world's hate drives them away from all hope in that quarter. God is greater than a world in arms.

III. This Is a Reason for Humility.

A. It strips the righteous of all pride in the fact of their being saved.

B. Of all exultation in self because they continue in their integrity.

C. Of all undue censure of the fallen; for they, themselves, would have failed had not the Lord upheld them.

D. Of all self-confidence as to the future, since their weakness is inherent and abiding.

E. Of all self-glorying, even in heaven, since in all things they are debtors to sovereign grace.

IV. This Is a Fruitful Ground of Hope.

A. In reference to our own difficulties; God can give us deliverance.

B. In reference to our tried brethren; the Lord can sustain, sanctify, and deliver them.

C. In reference to sinners; they cannot be too degraded, obstinate, ignorant, or false; God can work salvation even in the worst.

"SALVATION IS OF THE LORD" (Jonah 2:9). This is the sum of Jonah's discourse; one word for all; the very moral of his history. The mariners might have written upon their ship, instead of Castor and Pollux, or the like device, *Salvation is the Lord's*. The Ninevites in the next chapter might have written upon their gates, *Salvation is the Lord's*. All humankind whose cause is pitied and pleaded by God against the hardness of Jonah's heart, might have written in the palms of their hands, *Salvation is the Lord's*. It is the argument of both the Testaments, the staff and support of heaven and earth. They would both sink, and all their joints be severed, if the salvation of the Lord were not. —*King on* Jonah

THUS THE SAINTS hold heaven—not by conquest, but by heritage. Won by another arm than their own, it presents the strongest imaginable contrast to the spectacle in England's palace that day when the king demanded to know of his assembled nobles by what title they held their lands? What title! At the rash question a hundred swords leaped from their scabbards. Advancing on the alarmed monarch—"By these," they said, "we won, and by these will keep them."

How different the scene which heaven presents! All eyes are turned on Jesus with looks of love; gratitude glows in every bosom and swells every song. Now with golden harps they sound His praise. Now, descending from their thrones to do Him homage, they cast crowns in one glittering heap at the feet that were nailed on Calvary. From this scene, learn in whose name to seek salvation, and through whose merits to hope for it; and with a faith in harmony with the worship of the skies, be this your language—"Not unto us, O LORD, not unto us, but unto thy name give glory" (Ps. 115:1).
—*Guthrie*

"This brook will soon run dry," said one. "No," said his fellow companion, "it flows from a living spring, which was never known to fail in summer or in winter." A man was reputed to be very rich by those who saw his expensive houses, horses, and charges; but there were others who judged that his name would soon be in the *Gazette,* for he had no capital. "There is nothing at the back of it," said one, and the saying meant much. Now, the believer has the eternal deep for his spring of supply, and the all-sufficiency of God as the substance of his wealth. What cause has he to fear?

If salvation were partly of God and partly of man, it would be as sorry an affair as that image of Nebuchadnezzar's dream, which was partly of iron and partly of clay. It would end in a breakdown. If our dependence were upon Jesus, in a measure, and our own works in some degree, our foundation would be partly on the rock and partly on the sand, and the whole structure would fall. Oh, to know the full meaning of the words, *"Salvation is of the Lord."*

Experience alone can beat this truth into men's minds. A man will lie broken at the foot of the precipice, every bone dislocated by the fall, and yet hope to save himself. Piles of sin will fall upon him and bury him, and yet his self-trust will live. Mountains of actual transgression will overwhelm him, and yet he will stir himself to self-confident effort, working like the Cyclops which Etna heaped upon them. Crushed to atoms, every particle of our nature reeks with conceit. Ground to powder, our very dust is pungent with pride. Only the Holy Spirit can make a man receive that humbling sentence, *"Salvation is of the Lord."*

It will not save me to know that Christ is a Savior; but it will save me to trust Him to be my Savior. I shall not be delivered from the wrath to come by believing that His atonement is sufficient; but I shall be saved by making that atonement my trust, my refuge, and my all. The pith, the essence of faith lies in this—a casting of oneself on the promise. It is not the life jacket on board ship that saves the man when he is drowning, nor is it his belief that it is an excellent and successful invention. No! He must have it around him, or he will sink.

Spurgeon

THE HEAD OF A NATION
(INDEPENDENCE DAY)

Blessed is the nation whose God is the LORD; and the people whom he hath chosen for his own inheritance (Ps. 33:12).

Of the early days of our nation it may be said, as of the creation of the world, "In the beginning, God." And the most real and vital danger to our country is that we should depart from God in our national life and cease to own Him as Ruler.

1. True patriotism remembers that "righteousness exalteth a nation, but sin is a reproach to any people."

2. The true patriots are not the politicians who talk loudly about the flag and then rob the coffers of the nation. Those citizens are the real patriots who quietly and faithfully do their duty by the state and their fellow men, holding in reverence the laws and institutions of the land.

3. We should serve our nation for the kingdom's sake, and serve the kingdom for the nation's sake.

4. Love of country is born of God. Christians have always been patriots. Jesus loved His nation well enough to die for it. We are only fulfilling the law of the Lord when we give our country the deep, intelligent, and unswerving devotion of our hearts. The traitor to his nation is a traitor to God.

5. Patriotism is a sentiment that strikes down into the depths of a person's nature. It belongs to the inner recesses of the soul. It has to do with the most sacred sentiments. Men have ever linked it with the two other holy passions—love of family, and love of God. Thoughtful persons involuntarily associate patriotism with religion. In our own country this truth has been exemplified by the fact that many of the greatest patriots of our national history have been unequivocally Christian.

Selected

MEDITATION

While I was musing the fire burned (Ps. 39:3).

It is better to have too much than too little feeling in religion. We cannot love an unfeeling man. The feeling heart is the most human as well as the most humane part of humanity. But we admire it only when it leans upon a clear judgment and is thereby controlled.

There is much to be said in praise of quiet musing. We do not do much of it or see much of it in these days of rush and hurry. It has been said that meditation is a lost art. The order suggested here is musing, burning, speaking. "While I was musing the fire burned: then spake I with my tongue." Meditation is favorable to the most exalted feelings of devotion.

I. Some Proper Subjects of Meditation.
   A. The character of God.
   B. His providential dealings.
   C. The plan of salvation.
   D. Our relation to God.
   E. Our future.

II. Some Benefits of Meditation.
   A. The acquisition of religious power.
   B. The production of religious pleasure.
   C. The realization of religious hopes.

III. Meditation Is at Its Best.
   A. When it is a preparative for society and for action. We are the better fitted to go back again to our active duties and demands.
   B. We are made more kind, more gentle, more forbearing.
   C. In musing we are taught a more correct knowledge of ourselves than we should otherwise possess, and may thus be fitted to have more power to correctly appraise and give aid to our neighbor.

Hallock

A SOUL'S TALK WITH ITSELF

Psalm 42:5

1. The Controversy

Thirty years ago controversy waged around the question: Has man a soul? Today the question has changed from: Has man a soul? to, Is man a soul? The change is significant of much on both sides. It means that the materialist, pure and simple, has abandoned the old position.

Man has no soul; man is soul. The soul is the man. It is this soul quality that makes man a questioning, reasoning, and volitional being. In the mind, it is reason; in the heart, it is affection; in the will, it is determination. Man can question, love, and choose.

2. Self-Interrogation

Of all forms of questioning, self-questioning is the most important. No man ever talks with anyone more important than himself. No preaching is so far-reaching as the preaching to an audience of one, and that one the preacher himself. Every man has this strange power of projecting his personality and talking to himself. He can place himself outside himself, look his own soul straight in the face, and compel it to yield up its secret.

Look your soul in the face and force yourself to face ultimate issues. Am I saved or am I lost? Am I living for this life only, or for the infinite beyond? Am I content to cast God out of my life and live for the fleeting pleasures and glories of the world? Am I a wise man, or am I playing the fool? Ask yourself these things. An honest answer may decide a destiny.

3. Where Is Your God?

Questions cannot be ignored forever. Whether we question ourselves or not, others will force their questions upon us. Why? Where? What? How? These assail from every side. Questions—personal, pointed, and pertinent—challenge and confront us on the vital issues of life. Questions that perplex, unsettle, and challenge cannot be escaped.

The soul is apt to be overwhelmed and bowed down. Then is the time for the question: "Why art thou cast down, O my soul? and why art thou disquieted in me?" Challenge its moods. Get at the cause of depression and probe the roots of fear. A straight, simple question is often more than half the battle.

4. The Soul's Answer

Where is your God? That is an old question, and it is still being asked. Men have searched the heavens and ransacked the earth and cannot find Him. Where is He? Man has been analyzed, dissected, and vivisected, but no God can be found. Where is He? Where are the proofs of His presence when calamity and affliction overtake the sons of men? Where is God? Take the question to your own soul and ask it where He is. It is there you will find the answer.

Can you say, "He is the God of my life who fills my soul with peace and hears my prayer"?

Chadwick

I Found God

I found God in the dawning
   In the crimson flight of night,
In the notes of the birds at matins,
   In the sun-burst glory light.

I found Him in a garden,
   In the dew-drenched columbine,
In the shy and modest clinging
   Of the morning-glory vine.

I found Him in the patches
   Of the white clouds floating high,
That touched with animation
   The majestic vault of sky.

I found Him in a roadway,
   Through a quiet countryside,
And on a lake at sunset,
   Where the golden ripples ride.

At last in purple twilight
   In the cooling, fragrant air,
I heard God's presence whisper—
   I knew that He was there.

—Frank G. Weaver

THE CHRISTIAN'S HOPE

Hope thou in God (Ps. 42:5).

Hope is an essential. More so in seasons of darkness, depression, weakness.

I. The Thing That Is Here Urged—"Hope."

That is, expect all needful future good of every kind. Both in religious work and enjoyment. There is no limit to hope.

II. The Object of Hope Is Presented—"in God."

Not in self, not in men, but in God. He is the "God of hope." Christ, the Son, who is our hope. The Holy Spirit is the inspirer and sustainer of hope.

III. What Are Some of the Various Phases of Hope?

Similitudes are employed. "Anchor of the soul," in storms and perils. "Light of the soul," in darkness.

IV. Consider Some of the Many Reasons for This Hope:

A. God's ability and all-sufficiency.

B. His willingness to do all we need.

C. His changeless love—a great assurance and hope.

D. His precious promises—many, ample, sure. This hope in God is an imperative, glorious privilege, and an unspeakable duty and joy. "Hope thou in God."

Selected

WE ARE NOT ASHAMED of the ground of our hope. Our hope rests upon the solemn promises of God, which He made to us by His prophets and apostles, and confirmed in the person and work of His dear Son. Inasmuch as Jesus Christ died and rose from the dead, we who are one with Him by faith are sure that we shall rise again from the dead and live with Him. The fact of Christ's resurrection is the assurance of our resurrection, and His entrance into glory is the pledge of our glorification because we are made one with Him by the purpose and grace of God. As we fell in Adam by virtue of our being in him, so we rise and reign with Jesus because we are in Him. God is not the God of the dead, but of the living; yet is He the God of Abraham, of Isaac, and of Jacob, and therefore these men are yet alive. Even thus do we believe concerning all who die in the faith that they have not ceased to be, but they all live to Him. —*Spurgeon*

CHEER UP!

Why art thou cast down, O my soul? and why art thou disquieted within me? hope thou in God: for I shall yet praise him, who is the health of my countenance, and my God (Ps. 42:11).

I. **The Causes of Spiritual Despondency.**
   A. The burden of sin.
   B. The wickedness of the world.
   C. Earthly misfortunes.
   D. Bereavements.

II. **The Cure of Despondency.**
   A. A present trust in God.
   B. Looking to the future.

III. **The Reasons for Trust in God.**
   A. His present goodness to us.
   B. His revealed relation to us.

Selected

The Will of God

Thou sweet, beloved will of God,
　My anchor ground, my fortress hill,
My spirit's silent, fair abode,
　In Thee I hide me and am still.

Thy beautiful sweet will, my God,
　Holds fast in its sublime embrace
My captive will, a gladsome bird,
　Prison'd in such a realm of grace.

Upon God's will I lay me down,
　As child upon its mother's breast,
No silken couch, nor softest bed,
　Could ever give me such deep rest.

—Gerhardt Tersteegen

YET

. . . Hope in God; For I shall yet praise Him,
The help of my countenance and my God (Ps. 42:11 NKJV).

The connecting words are "I shall yet praise him." "Yet!" Look at it! Listen to it! What a grip it has! How impossible to beat it off! How it fans a spark to a flame! How it goes on through difficulty! How it holds fast in trial! How it glows in darkness! How tireless it is! Yet! Yet! "I shall yet praise him!"

1. **The present must not overwhelm you.** Today must not claim your surrender. Do not measure your life by that little eddy we call "now." "I shall yet praise him."

2. **Give me faith, and I can live and wait.** I preach a faith that will forever declare, "Maybe I can't praise him just now and here, but I will yet do so!" The storm by its fierceness is driving me nearer home. Then I will hold the rudder firm. I will watch every cloud in defiance. I will sing at every raging sea, "I shall yet praise him!"

3. **I might as well begin now.**

Selected

WE ARE READY to praise when all shines fair. But when life is overcast, when all things seem to be against us, when we are in fear for some cherished happiness, or in the depths of sorrow, or in the solitude of a life that has no visible support, or in a season of sickness, and with the shadow of death approaching—then to praise God? Then to say, This fear, loneliness, affliction, pain, and trembling awe are as sure tokens of love as life, health, joy, and the gifts of home? "The Lord gave, and the Lord hath taken away"; on either side it is He, and all is love alike. "Blessed be the name of the Lord"—this is the true sacrifice of praise. What can come amiss to a soul that is so in accord with God? What can make so much as one jarring tone in all its harmony? In all the changes of this fitful life, it ever dwells in praise.

—H. E. Manning

ESSENTIALS FOR SOULWINNING

Create in me a clean heart, O God. . . .
Restore unto me the joy of thy salvation . . . (Ps. 51:10–13).

I. **Cleanliness (v. 10).**
   A. "Create in me a clean heart."
   B. "Renew a right spirit within me."

II. **Communion (v. 11)**
   A. "Cast me not away from thy presence."
   B. "Take not thy holy spirit from me."

III. **Constancy (v. 12)**
   A. "Restore unto me the joy of thy salvation."
   B. "Uphold me with thy free spirit."

IV. **Compassion (v. 13)**
   A. "Then will I teach transgressors thy ways."
   B. "Sinners shall be converted unto thee."

Richard Mullin

Who Does the Winning?

I tried to win a soul for Christ;
   How earnestly I pleaded
That he had sinned and gone astray
   And Christ was all he needed.
I begged him to forsake the world,
   Repent and be forgiven—
I tried to coax him to the Lord,
   To woo him into Heaven.
And then I realized that Christ
   Longed for him more than I,
That He alone could make one care,
   Who cared enough to die.
Upon my knees I fought the fight—
My friend was born again that night.

—Barbara E. Cornet

THE JOY OF SALVATION

Restore unto me the joy of thy salvation;
and uphold me with thy free spirit (Ps. 51:12).

I. **Salvation Begets Joy**
   A. The joy of reconciliation.
   B. The joy of possession.
   C. The joy of anticipation.

II. **This Joy Is Lost by Indulgence in Sin**
   A. The Christian sometimes falls into sin.
   B. No man can sin and retain his peace of mind.
   C. The departure of joy leaves a vacancy in the heart.

III. **Joy Will Be Restored upon True Repentance**
   What is true repentance? Not simply fear of punishment; but grief at having broken God's law, and grieved God's Spirit; combined with a desire to live a nobler, purer life. Forgiveness cannot be obtained while sin is retained.

F. J. Austin

WHERE DOES JOY come from? I knew a Sunday school student whose conception of joy was that it was a thing made in lumps and kept somewhere in heaven, and that when people prayed for it pieces were somehow let down and fitted into their souls. I am not sure that views as gross and material are not often held by people who ought to be wiser. In reality, joy is as much a matter of cause and effect as pain. No one can get joy by merely asking for it. It is one of the ripest fruits of the Christian life, and, like all fruits, must be grown. —*Henry Drummond*

Joy

Joy is a fruit that will not grow
   In nature's barren soil;
All we can boast, till Christ we know,
   Is vanity and toil.
But where the Lord hath planted grace,
   And made His glories known,
These fruits of heavenly joy and peace
   Are found, and there alone.

—*John Newton*

THE SALVATION OF GOD
(LENT)

Psalm 51:12

1. The Author of Salvation. The Lord Jesus (Heb. 5:9).

2. The Way of Salvation. Through faith (Acts 14:27).

3. The Knowledge of Salvation. By the Word (Luke 1:77).

4. The Joy of Salvation. In the believers (Ps. 51:12).

5. The Day of Salvation. Now (2 Cor. 6:2).

Salvation is of the Lord. For all who believe. The knowledge of it comes by believing the Word, and the joy of it follows.

Selected

I Have Found It!

I have found the perfect treasure,
   Richer than my fondest dream;
It is mine and mine forever,
   Safe from every selfish scheme.

Wealth as vast as all of heaven!
   Beauty fairer than the day!
Joy with no corrupting leaven
   Shall go with me all the way!

Long I sought this wondrous blessing,
   Sought by labor under law,
Till God's grace reached down, caressing,
   Touched my faith—and then I saw!

Will you share with me this treasure
   Gift of God's amazing grace?
'Twill be more than all earth's measure
   Just to look upon His face!

—L. M. Hearn

TOGETHERNESS AMONG CHRISTIANS

We took sweet counsel together, and walked unto the house of God in company (Ps. 55:14).

Togetherness, cooperation, should characterize Christians.

1. **This should be true in our worship.**

    Private worship and radio worship have their value, but there is no substitute for public worship. "Forsake not the assembling of yourselves together."

2. **This should be true in our social life.**

    It has been well said, "The more we get together, the happier we will be." Togetherness is a great source of comfort and joy.

3. **Togetherness should characterize our financial support of the church.**

    "On the first day of the week let every one of you lay by him in store as God has prospered." What great things we can do when we put our hearts and our hands together!

4. **Togetherness should characterize our warfare and our work for Christ.**

    Christian soldiers must not be divided, scattered. We are strong to do exploits when united.

There is great safety and mutual helpfulness in togetherness. Among the mountains of Switzerland, where the difficulties and dangers of travelers are great, they have a way of binding a group of adventurers together. Before they commence the slippery and perilous ascent, a strong cord is bound around the waist of each, and all are then tied together. Thus everyone helps the others. If one slips, the others pull that person up again.

Just so helpful have the ties of Christian church relationships been found by multitudes of members as they have felt the uplift of mutual sympathy, the vitality of united effort, and the inspiration of a common purpose and affection. And there are difficulties enough in the Christian life that we really need all the help we can get. By every means let us promote togetherness among Christians.

Hallock

"OTHER REFUGE HAVE I NONE"

God is a refuge for us (Ps. 62:8).

Christians possess advantage of which unbelievers seem to be ignorant. When visited by calamity they have an unfailing Refuge in God.

1. Our Need of the Divine Refuge.

Sensible of our sin and guilt, and of our helplessness to deliver ourselves, we need and know no other refuge but God. Though the believer may know himself delivered from guilt and condemnation, he is still aware that he is not finally delivered. He dwells in a corrupt world. He still dwells in a body of sin and death. He feels deeply his need of such a refuge as God is. On account of the conflict he must wage, in his own heart and with the world, he needs a refuge.

Not only is there sin to contend with, but no believer can be free from tribulation. "Man is born to trouble as the sparks fly upward." "Many are the afflictions of the righteous"—personal losses, poverty, family bereavements, the slander and persecutions of human tongues—all these the Christian is subject to. He needs a refuge. God is his refuge and strength. "Other refuge have I none."

2. The Nature of This Refuge—the Kind of Refuge God Is.

A refuge is a place of safe retreat, of shelter. It is a place of escape from danger, where one can find protection from the pursuit of an enemy. In Old Testament times there were appointed "cities of refuge." God is such a refuge. Think of His excellency as a refuge, suitable, strong, effectual, easy of access, unfailing. When sensible of sin and guilt, in time of conflict, in tribulation, in affliction, "Other refuge have I none; hangs my helpless soul on Thee!"

3. To Enjoy This Refuge We Must Flee to It.

We must be in it. To be only near is of no avail. When we take refuge in God, He will give us grace to fight a good war, to conquer the world.

Hallock

"ELOHIM"

Psalm 62

God is mentioned seven times in the above Psalm. As it occurs in the plural, in the Christian sense as read in the reflected light of the Scriptures, it denotes the Father, Son, and the Holy Spirit in their united action of power.

1. **Salvation.** "God: from him cometh my salvation" (v. 1).

2. **Expectation.** "God; for my expectation is from him" (v. 5).

3. **Protection.** "In God is my salvation and my glory" (v. 7).

4. **Power.** "The rock of my strength, and my refuge, is in God" (v. 7).

5. **Safety.** "God is a refuge for us" (v. 8).

6. **Revelation.** "God hath spoken" (v. 11).

7. **Possession.** "Power belongeth unto God" (v. 11).

F. E. Marsh

O God of the impossible!
　Since all things are to Thee
But soil in which Omnipotence
　Can work almightily,

Each trial may to us become
　The means that will display
How o'er what seems impossible
　Our God holds perfect sway!

The very storms that beat upon
　Our little barque so frail,
But manifest Thy power to quell
　All forces that assail.

The things that are too hard for us
　The foes that are too strong,
Are just the very ones that may
　Awake a triumph song.

O God of the impossible,
　When we no hope can see,
Grant us the faith that still believes
　ALL possible to Thee!

—Author Unknown

RIVERS OF GOD
(SPRINGTIME)

The river of God, which is full of water (Ps. 65:9).

The river of God—a stream whose sources are hidden in the bosom of the eternal hills. Fed by the pure snows of heaven. Its growing volume. The continuity of the stream. The course of the river has windings and vicissitudes. But abundance—the whole tone of God's sanctuary is abundance. If we die of thirst it is our own responsibility.

1. **Here Is a River Unlike Any Other.**
   It is pure, clean, deep, sweet, satisfying, ceaseless.

2. **Here Is a River Greater Than Our Need.**
   Who can number the drops of rain?

3. **Here Is a River Greater Than Our Capacity.**
   Where does God economize in His care for us?

4. **Here Is a River "Full of Water."**
   You can satisfy your thirst here. "There is a river, the streams whereof shall make glad the city of God" (Ps. 46:4). Drink. Give thanks.

Selected

O Love of God most full,
O Love of God most free,
Come warm my heart, come fill my soul,
Come lead me unto Thee!

Warm as the glowing sun
So shines Thy love on me,
It wraps me 'round with kindly care,
It draws me unto Thee.

The wildest sea is calm,
The tempest brings no fear,
The darkest night is full of light,
Because Thy love is near.

I triumph over sin,
I put temptation down;
The love of God doth give me strength
To win the victor's crown.

—Oscar Clute

"LEAD ME"; "TEACH ME"

Psalm 25:5

I. **The Prevalent Pleader.**
"Lead me."
   A. *His character shown by the prayer*:
      1. *Humility.* "Lead me," I feel I cannot walk alone. "Teach me," I feel my ignorance.
      2. *His wisdom.* He prays for the best things, uses the chiefest argument.
      3. *His faith.* "I wait," evidently expecting an answer.
      4. *His patience.* "I wait"; he had waited long, but is willing to wait God's time.
   B. *His behavior*:
      1. *He prays and waits.* Thus God is honored.
      2. *He waits and prays.* Thus his anxiety is demonstrated.

II. **The Twofold Prayer.**
"Lead me"; "teach me."

A. *Lead me:* Help me to walk according to Your revealed will.

B. *Teach me:* Your leading may be contrary to my expectation—for joy, I may have bitterness; for a wealthy place, a desert. Teach me of Your wisdom and faithfulness that I may praise You and declare Your righteousness.

Although a child of God is content when his Father sees fit to lead him blindfold, yet his desire is to see, as well as believe, "The goodness of the Lord in the land of the living."

III. **The Manifold Argument.**
"Thou art the God of my salvation." How suitably has the psalmist ordered his case. For—

A. The Savior has engaged to keep the saved. More emphatically than Ruth has the Lord said to His people, "I will never leave thee," etc.

B. The Savior has promised to teach. Jesus in after days said that He would send the Spirit to lead us into all truth.

C. The Savior has revealed His desire that the redeemed should recognize and celebrate His faithfulness.

D. He who could put our feet in the right path will surely guide our steps therein.

E. He who loves us enough to save us will surely answer our cry for guidance and teaching.

Stems and Twigs

THE SEED AND ITS HARVEST

There shall be an handful of corn in the earth upon the top of the mountains; the fruit thereof shall shake like Lebanon: and they of the city shall flourish like grass of the earth (Ps. 72:16).

In these words are suggested:

I. The Seeming Insignificance of the Gospel in Its Origin.
It is just a seed, some "corn."

A. Apparent insignificance in its introduction into the world.

B. In its structure as a system of religion.

C. In its operation on the heart. Silent, often unnoticed.

II. The Previous Improbability of Its Success.

A. There was powerful opposition to be encountered from the native enmity of the human heart, from long-established forms of error, from the spirit of the age, and from the influence of the Evil One.

B. A feeble agency was employed—lack of eloquence, power, wealth.

III. Its Stupendous Results.
"Fruit shall shake like Lebanon."

A. The number of its converts.

B. Their graces.

C. Their influence. "Thy kingdom come" (Matt. 6:10; Luke 11:2).

Selected

ALL MEN SHALL BE BLESSED IN HIM

*His name shall endure for ever: his name shall be continued
as long as the sun: and men shall be blessed in him:
all nations shall call him blessed (Ps. 72:17).*

I. **The Renown Which the Savior Shall Acquire.**
   The sources from which it is derived.
   A. It is derived from the constitution of His person.
   B. It is derived from His work.
   C. It is derived from His reward.

II. **The Influence Which the Savior Shall Exert.**
   The duration through which it shall last.
   A. Its beneficial nature.
   B. Its universal extent.
   C. Its unworldly methods.

Selected

The Conquering Son

O North, with all thy vales of green!
O South, with all thy palms!
From peopled towns and fields
    between
  Uplift the voice of psalms.
Raise ancient East, the anthem high,
And let the youthful West reply.

Lo! in the clouds of heaven appears
  God's well-beloved Son;
He brings a train of brighter years;
  His kingdom is begun.
He comes a guilty world to bless
With mercy, truth, and righteousness.

O Father! haste the promised hour,
  When at His feet shall lie
All rule, authority, and power,
  Beneath the ample sky:
When He shall reign from pole to pole,
The Lord of every human soul:

When all shall heed the words He said,
  Amid their daily cares,
And, by the loving life He led,
  Shall strive to pattern theirs;
And He, who conquered Death, shall
  win
The mightier conquest over sin.

—*William Cullen Bryant*

CAN GOD, THE ALMIGHTY, BE LIMITED?

And [they] limited the Holy One of Israel (Ps. 78:41).

God's wise and benevolent purposes are often frustrated. There are many things God would do for men if permitted.

1. **Inconsistent Christian living limits God.** "Your iniquities have separated" (Isa. 59:2). "Your sins have withholden" (Jer. 5:25).

2. **Lack of faith limits God.** We limit the Holy One of Israel by distrust. Jesus at Nazareth "did not many mighty works there because of their unbelief" (Matt. 13:58). Many of us lack an adventurous faith. We are afraid to "launch out into the deep" (Luke 5:4). When you say, "My sins are too many to be forgiven," you have limited God. You have put your sins above His grace.

3. **Shallow and selfish prayers limit God.** They restrict Him. "Ye ask, and receive not, because ye ask amiss" (James 4:3). See the parable of the Pharisee and the publican. We often limit God by the narrowness of our prayers. Also by our lack of praying.

4. **A stubborn will limits God.** "He came to his own, and his own received him not" (John 1:11). "O Jerusalem, Jerusalem . . . how often would I have gathered thy children . . . and ye would not" (Matt. 23:37).

To limit God is to set bounds to His operations, to circumscribe or confine Him in His ability to effect certain purposes or works. The penitent sinner often does this when he doubts God's willingness and ability to save. The Christian in trouble often does this in confining God to a certain mode of deliverance. God extends His gifts, but we must accept them. Jesus invites us to come, but He can't compel us to come. Jesus stands at the door and knocks, but we must open the door. The key is on our side.

Selected

SPARROWS AND SWALLOWS

Yea, the sparrow hath found an house, and the swallow a nest for herself, where she may lay her young, even thine altars, O Lᴏʀᴅ of hosts, my King, and my God (Ps. 84:3).

David, as an exile, envied the birds that dwelt around the house of the Lord. So the Christian, when debarred from the assembly of the saints or under spiritual desertion, will pine to be once more at home with God.

These birds found in the sanctuary what we would find in God.

I. Houses for Themselves.

    A. Consider what they were. Sparrows.
- Worthless creatures. Five for two farthings.
- Needy creatures, requiring both nests, food, and everything else.
- Numerous creatures; but none were driven away.

    B. Consider what they enjoyed:
- Safety.
- Rest.   All this in the house of God, near
- Abode.   His altars. Thus do believers find all
- Delight. *in Christ Jesus.*
- Society.
- Nearness.

It is not every bird that does this. The eagle is too ambitious. The vulture too filthy. The cormorant too greedy. The hawk too warlike. The ostrich too wild. The domestic fowl too dependent upon man. The owl too fond of darkness.

These sparrows were little and loving.

II. Nests for Their Young.

Children should be housed in the house of God. The sanctuary of God should be the nursery of the young.

    A. They will be safe there, and free there. The swallow, the "bird of liberty," is satisfied to find a nest for herself near the altars of God. She is not afraid of bondage there either for herself or her young.

    B. They will be joyful there. We should try to make our little ones happy in God, and in His holy worship.

C. They are likely to return to the nest, as the swallows do; even as the young salmon return to the rivulet where they were hatched. Young folks remember their first impressions.

D. Children truly brought to Christ have every blessing in that fact.

- They are rich; they dwell in God's palace.
- They are educated; they abide in the Lord's Temple.
- They are safe for time and eternity.

Are you sighing after Christ for yourself and your children? Are you content without Christ? Then you are not likely to care about your children. Do you already possess a home in Jesus? Rest not until all yours are housed in the same place.

Sir Thomas More used to attend the parish church at Chelsea, and there putting on a surplice, he would sing with the choristers at matins and high mass. It happened, one day, that the Duke of Norfold coming to Chelsea to dine with him, found him at church thus engaged. As they walked home together arm in arm after service the duke exclaimed, "My Lord Chancellor a parish clerk! A parish clerk! you dishonor the king and his office!" "Nay," he replied, smiling, "your Grace cannot suppose that the king, our master, will be offended with me for serving his Master, or thereby account his office dishonored."

"God fails not," as one has beautifully said, "to find a house for the most *worthless,* and the nest for the most *restless* of birds." What confidence this should give us! How we should rest!
—*Things New and Old*

As a rule, the children of godly parents are godly. In cases where this is not the case there is a reason. I have carefully observed and detected the absence of family prayer, gross inconsistency, harshness, indulgence, or neglect of admonition. If trained in God's ways, they do not depart from them.

Spurgeon

GOD OUR STRENGTH

Psalm 84:5

1. Power belongeth to God (Ps. 62:11; 93:4; Nah. 1:3).

2. He controls the sea (Job 38:11; Jer. 5:22).

3. He stills the tempests (Ps. 65:7; Matt. 8:26; 14:32).

4. He rules the elements (Ps. 148:8; Prov. 30:4).

5. God can do all things (Job 42:2; Matt. 19:26).

6. The power given to His Son (Acts 10:38; Rom. 1:4).

7. Through Him we get the victory (Eph. 3:16; Col. 1:11–12).

Selected

GOD IS MERCIFUL

Psalm 86:5

1. His mercy is eternal (Ps. 103:17; 106:1).

2. It moves us to repentance (Joel 2:13; Rom. 2:4).

3. It makes salvation possible (Lam. 3:22; Titus 3:5).

4. It is the source of our forgiveness (Mic. 7:18; Eph. 2:4, 8).

5. It is the basis of our hope (Ps. 130:7; 147:11).

6. It is offered to repentant sinners (Ps. 32:5; Prov. 28:13; Luke 15:18–20).

Selected

NUMBERING OUR DAYS
(NEW YEAR)

So teach us to number our days, that we may apply our hearts unto wisdom (Ps. 90:12).

There is a tendency in men to neglect to form a true estimate of life. "All men think all men mortal but themselves." The formation of a right judgment in this matter is essential to practical wisdom. This is a psalm of life and death, and one of the finest in the Bible. The comparisons made between the frailty and brevity of human life and the omnipotence and eternity of God are very striking. But the right use of the sense of mortality is a priceless blessing.

I. Our days are numbered.
A. They are few. Life at its longest is brief.

B. They are fleet. They speed away.

C. They are uncertain. "Boast not thyself of tomorrow" (Prov. 27:1).

D. The sure evidence is in the prevalence of mortality around us.

II. Because of the brevity of life we should use our time wisely.
"I must work the works of him that sent me, while it is day: the night cometh, when no man can work" (John 9:4). "So teach us to number our days," etc. Said a thoughtful man: "I have but one life to live; if I invest it unworthily my regret will be as long as eternity."

III. The Teacher to whom we should apply.
It is God Himself. How does God teach? In many ways, by parents, ministers, friends, and in many outward events.

IV. The end of God's teaching.
"That we may apply our hearts unto wisdom." Man is dangerously apt to forget this numbering. He allows the days to slip away unnoticed. He numbers other men's days, but not his own. And we must also number our nights, with their blessings of rest and repose and renewal, for human life is incomplete without the night as well as the day.

Hallock

OUR DAYS ARE NUMBERED
(NEW YEAR)

So teach us to number our days, that we may apply our hearts unto wisdom (Ps. 90:12).

I. **The Duty Suggested.** "Number our days."
    A. Number their fewness.
    B. Number their fleetness.
    C. Number their uncertainty.

II. **The Prayer Inspired.** "So teach us to number."
    A. Suggested by the flight of the seasons.
    B. By the prevalence of mortality around us.
    C. By the lessons of the Scriptures.
    D. By the influence of the Holy Spirit.

III. **The End to Be Attained.** "That we may apply our hearts unto wisdom."

A. That we may apply our hearts vigorously. That is what "apply" means.

B. That we may apply our hearts immediately. Yes, no delay. The immediate duty, and very desirable of performance.

Selected

My Only Plea

Just one thing, O Master, I ask today,
Now that the old year has passed away
And a promising new year, thro' grace of Thine,
With all the dreams of youth is mine—
Just one thing I ask as I onward go,

That I'll walk with Thee—not too fast, nor slow;
Just one thing I ask and nothing more,
Not to linger behind, nor run before.
O Master! This is my only plea—
Take hold of my life and pilot me.

—Walter J. Kuhn

LIFE FLEETING
(NEW YEAR)

So teach us to number our days,
that we may apply our hearts unto wisdom (Ps. 90:12).

I.   The Proper Estimate of Life.
A. It is temporary.
B. It is preparative.

II.   The Tendency to Neglect the Computation.
A. Secular concerns.
B. Repugnance to death.
C. Dread of the future.

III.   The Wisdom of Right Estimate.
A. It will moderate our earthly affections.
B. It will reconcile us to our earthly afflictions.
C. It will stimulate us to heavenly devotion.

Selected

God's Will

I asked the New Year for some motto sweet,
Some rule of life by which to guide my feet,
I asked and paused; it answered soft and low,
   "God's will to *know*."

Will knowledge then suffice? New Year, I cried,
But ere the question into silence died
The answer came, "No, this remember too,
   God's will to *do*."

Once more I asked, is there still more to tell?
And once again the answer sweetly fell;
"Yes, this one thing all other things above,
   God's will to *love*."

—Author Unknown

ANGELIC PROTECTION IN APPOINTED WAYS

For he shall give his angels charge over thee,
to keep thee in all thy ways (Ps. 91:11).

We are pilgrims on our way to Canaan. He who set us free by the Passover deliverance also provides for our journey to the land that flows with milk and honey. All the way to the promised land is covered by this divine safe conduct.

I. There Are Ways Which Are Not in the Promise.

"All thy ways" are mentioned; but some tracks are not to be followed by children of God, and are not their ways.

A. Ways of presumption. In these men court danger, and, as it were defy God. "Cast thyself down," said Satan to our Lord, and then urged this promise (Matt. 4:6).

B. Ways of sin, dishonesty, lying, vice, worldly conformity, etc. We have no permit to bow in the house of Rimmon (Eph. 5:12; 2 Kings 5:18).

C. Ways of worldliness, selfishness, greed, ambition. The ways by which men seek personal aggrandizement are usually dark and crooked and are not of God (Prov. 28:22; 1 Tim. 6:9).

D. Ways of independence, willfulness, obstinacy, fancy, day-dreaming, absurd impulse, etc. (Jer. 2:18).

E. Ways of erroneous doctrine, novel practice, fashionable ceremony, flattering delusion, etc. (2 Tim. 3:5).

II. There Are Ways in Which Safety Is Guaranteed.

A. The way of humble faith in the Lord Jesus.

B. The way of obedience to divine precepts.

C. The way of childlike trust in providential guidance.

D. The way of strict principle and stern integrity.

E. The way of consecrated service and seeking God's glory.

F. The way of holy separation and walking with God.

III. These Ways Lead Us into Varied Conditions.

A. They are changeful and varied; "all thy ways."

B. They are sometimes stony with difficulty; "foot against a stone."

C. They may be terrible with temptation.

D. They may be mysteriously trying. Devils may throng the path—only to be met by holy angels.

E. They are essentially safe, while the smooth and easy roads are perilous.

IV. But While Walking in Them All Believers Are Secure.

A. The Lord Himself concerns Himself about them. "He shall give His angels charge over *thee*." He will personally command those holy beings to have an eye to His children. David charged his troops to spare Absalom, but his bidding was disregarded. It is not so with God.

B. Each one is *personally* watched over. "Charge over *thee*, to keep *thee*" (see Isa. 42:8; Gen. 28:15).

C. That watchfulness is perpetual—"*All* thy ways" (see Ps. 121:3–4).

D. All this comes to them by Jesus, whose the angels are, and whom they serve (see Isa. 43:4).

How cheerfully we should watch over others! How vigorously should we hold them up whenever it is in our power! To cast off a stumbling brother is not angelic, but the reverse.

While King William, at a battle in Flanders, was giving orders in the thickest of the fight, he saw, to his surprise, among his staff one Michael Godfrey—a merchant of London and Deputy Governor of the Bank of England—who had thus exposed himself in order to gratify his curiosity. The king, riding up to him, said, "Sir, you ought not to run these hazards; you are not a soldier, you can be of no use here." "Sire," answered Godfrey, "I run no more hazard than your Majesty." "Not so," said William. "I am here where it is my duty to be, and I may, without presumption, commit my life to God's keeping. But you—" The sentence needed no completion, for at that very moment a cannon ball laid Godfrey lifeless at the king's feet. He had been wise had he restricted himself to the ways of his calling and duty.

A dying saint asked that his name should be put upon his tombstone with the dates of his birth and death, and the one word, "*Kept*."

No angel will give in his account with sorrow, saying, "I could not keep him; the stones were too many, his feet too feeble, the way too long." No, we shall be kept to the end. For in addition to angels, we have the safeguard of their Lord. "He will keep the feet of his saints" (1 Sam. 2:9).

Spurgeon

PALM-TREE CHRISTIANS
(PALM SUNDAY)

The righteous shall flourish like the palm tree. . . . (Ps. 92:12–15).

On Palm Sunday palm branches may honor Christ, as at His triumphal entry; but palm-tree Christians honor Him all the year round.

If ever there were "tongues in trees," there is one in the palm tree—"prince of the vegetable kingdom," "the blest tree," and "the sister of man," as it has been called.

The emphatic word, which is thrice repeated, is *flourish*. Palm-tree Christians "flourish." And the psalmist proceeds to indicate wherein they flourish, namely, in a wealth of life, in a variety of serviceableness, and in a persistency that survives the years.

1. The palm is distinguished for its rich, stalwart life. It is a life that triumphs over the hard conditions of the desert. As by magic, it can so change the elements found in the unkindly soil around it as to make them minister to its growth and strength and fruitfulness.

2. The palm is further distinguished for the variety of its serviceableness. It "flourished" as embellishment in the temple of old, both in structure and furniture. As a living tree, it yielded oil, wine, and honey, or palm sugar, thus contributing to illumination, health, and comfort. In the desert its tall plume of bright verdure, perpetually green, is a far-seen signal, announcing to the desert ranger a place where shade and rest and water can be found.

3. But the palm "flourishes" in nothing more than in a persistency of life and service that defies the years, that knows no old age, that perpetuates an essential youth.

Now, suffice it to say, more by suggestion than enlargement, the "flourish" note is needed. Too many lives languish, droop, and trail. They are anemic, moribund. What service can such lives render either in "the courts of our God," or in the open desert world? The call is for more "planting" of the palm in "the house of the Lord."

Selected

FEDERATED THANKSGIVING
(THANKSGIVING)

Let us come before his presence with thanksgiving (Ps. 95:2).

You are an individual, but you are also a member of society. Community thanksgiving is the voice of the church.

1. We thank God for life and health. These we share together. When plague strikes a city, terror reigns. Thank God for conscious well-being and supply of daily needs.

2. We are thankful for the benefits of civilization, for ordered government, for scientific improvements, for education, good streets, institutions of benevolence, industry, and art. America has done much to improve the lot of the common men and women like ourselves. We must share it with the world.

3. We are thankful for a Christian environment where temperance and goodwill are encouraged, and fellowship with kindly folk is possible for us all. What would we be without the church, the open Bible, and the Gospel of Christ? These are values beyond man's power to estimate.

4. We are thankful for faith in the midst of tragedy. There is a God who understands and cares. Dark and mysterious is our life, but His way is good and true. Our trust is in our salvation.

5. We are grateful for the vision of better things to be, for the promise of Christ's kingdom and universal brotherhood in Him. It is our highway from despair, cynicism, and degeneracy.

6. We thank God for the hope eternal. This life is but the seed of a life that will blossom into unimaginable glory according to the promise of God.

Selected

"OUR GOD" IN THE PSALMS

He is our God; and we are his people (Ps. 95:7).

1. **Rock** of His Personality. "Who is a rock save our God?" (18:31; see 48:14; 113:5).

2. **Refuge** of His Defense. "In the name of our God we will set up our banners" (20:5).

3. **Remembrancer** for Our Thought. "Remember the name of the LORD our God" (20:7).

4. **Returner** to Adjust. "Our God shall come, and shall not keep silent" (50:3; see 44:21; 99:8; 105:7).

5. **Regarder** to Bless. "Our own God shall bless us" (67:6; see 123:2).

6. **Object** of Worship. "Exalt ye the LORD our God" (99:5, 9; see 147:1, 7).

7. **Embodiment** of Holiness. "The LORD our God is holy" (99:9).

8. **Source** of Salvation. "Save us, O LORD our God" (106:47; see 98:3).

F. E. Marsh

O God, our help in ages past,
    Our hope in years to come,
Our shelter from the stormy blast,
    And our eternal home—

Under the shadow of thy throne
    Thy saints have dwelt secure;
Sufficient is thine arm alone,
    And our defense is sure. . . .

Our God, our help in ages past,
    Our hope in years to come,
Be thou our guard while troubles last,
    And our eternal home.

—Isaac Watts

BRING AN OFFERING
(GIVING)

Bring an offering, and come into his courts (Ps. 96:8).

Ordinarily we think of worship as an assembly at an hour and place set aside for song, prayer, responses, liturgies, sermons, and the "taking of a collection." Is the "collection" an integral part of worship? Has it the spiritual significance of, for example, prayer, reading of Scripture, and a hymn? Why come into His courts with an offering?

I. **Giving of material gifts is associated with worship all through the Scriptures.** "Honor the Lord with thy substance" (Prov. 3:9), etc.

A. The story of Cain and Abel.

B. The story of Melchizedek.

C. Example of the temple worship.

D. "On the first day of the week (the day of public worship) let each one of you lay by him in store," etc.

II. **We bring our gifts as part of worship.**

A. Not to appease God. "Will the Lord be pleased with thousands of rams?" (Mic. 6:7), etc.

B. Not to enrich Him. "The world is [his], and the fullness thereof" (Ps. 50:12). But to acknowledge His ownership. To confess our dependence upon Him. As an expression of our gratitude. Every offering is a "thank offering." As a pledge of the sincerity of our faith. As a dedication of ourselves. Wealth is coined personality. And to keep the springs of our generosity from becoming dry or bitter. Why is the Dead Sea dead? Because it receives and never gives. Why be a Dead-Sea Christian?

All this is involved in giving as an act of worship. So come and bring an offering!

Selected

THE EAGLE-LIKE CHRISTIAN

So that thy youth is renewed like the eagle's (Ps. 103:5).

Commenting on these words, "Thy youth is renewed like the eagle's," the late Rev. John Henry Jowett paid a beautiful tribute to a deacon of his church. Though he was an old man, he called him "the youngest deacon in my church, always a child of the morning" and interested in every forward-looking work. He said: "I have never heard him speak about sunsets. He is a child of God; his youth is renewed every day; he will die with his face to the east, looking for the morning." Such is the eagle-like Christian.

1. The eagle is the emblem of the mature Christian in the penetration of its eye.

2. The eagle is the emblem of the mature Christian in the elevation of its flight.

3. The eagle is the emblem of the mature Christian in the swiftness of its motion.

4. The eagle is the emblem of the mature Christian in the dignity of its appearance.

5. You cannot tell how old a person is by the number of years he or she has lived.

We have known persons youthful in disposition at eighty years of age. Louis II, King of Hungary, died of old age at twenty. Haydn's oratorio, "The Creation," was composed by him at seventy. Humboldt wrote his immortal work, "The Cosmos," at seventy-five. Titian was engaged on his greatest painting when he died in his one hundredth year.

Selected

SIN

Psalm 103:12

Introduction

    A. Sin is the most vital issue facing the psalmist and man.

    B. We study sin to understand from whence we were saved, to continue in humility, and to prevent falling into it again.

I. Sin Is Twofold

    A. Being (51:5).

        1. A universal penalty of the fall of man.

        2. An inner condition of sin.

    B. Functioning (51:3).

        1. Personal free-moral agency and responsibility.

        2. Functioning—acquired in living this life sinfully.

II. What Is a Sin?

    A. A transgression of a known law of God (32:5; 51:4).

    B. Spiritual death, legal guilt, moral disease.

    C. We are not to sin (4:4; 39:1).

III. The Cure for Sins or Functioning Sinfully

    A. Conviction (38:3b).

    B. Confession (32:5a).

    C. Repentance and sorrow for sin (38:18).

    D. Effective faith (51:2).

Conclusion

    A. God can forgive sin (103:12).

    B. God's Word is the insurance against sinning (119:11).

    C. Such a state of forgiveness is blessedness (32:1).

Gene Mallory

LEANNESS OF SOUL

He gave them their request; but sent leanness into their soul
(Ps. 106:15).

Bent supremely on earthly desires the soul withers, dries up, becomes a lean and miserable thing.

1. Many things good in themselves may not be good for us individually.

2. Many things good for us at one time may not be good for us at another time and under other circumstances.

3. The most fervent prayers are not always the most acceptable. Some are passionate, selfish.

4. God may grant the passionate desire of a selfish heart with harm to the person. Such the text instances. Evil of unsubmissive requests.

5. God may refuse to grant the request of even a good man, and the refusal be a blessing. Paul's "thorn."

6. The wisest, most acceptable prayer is for conformity to the will of God. Christ in Gethsemane: "Thy will, not mine."

Selected

SAY SO

Let the redeemed of the Lord say so (Ps. 107:2).

This exhortation is not to glorify ourselves or what we have done, but to tell what God has done; and not what He has done for us physically, mentally or socially, though all of these are worthy of sacred praise, but what He has done for us spiritually. He has redeemed us.

1. This duty we owe to ourselves. No true man is willing to compromise himself, but is ready for the world to know where he stands.

2. This duty of letting others know we are redeemed we owe also to others. The secret disciple wins few for his Master.

3. This duty of letting others know that we are redeemed we owe, above all else, to God. We owe it as a matter of gratitude. We owe it as a matter of rejoicing. All the honor and all the praise of our salvation belong to our God. We owe it to Him as a matter of obedience. He commands it. "Let the redeemed of the Lord say so."

4. We who are redeemed should "say so" in word—both written and spoken. Many souls have been won to Christ by written appeal. We should "say so" with spoken word, both in personal profession as we publicly own Jesus as our Savior, and also by personal testimony. Like Andrew we must go and find others and bring them to Jesus.

5. We who are redeemed should "say so" by our works—not only by the words of our lips, but also by the works of our lives. Here, too, "actions speak louder than words." The Gospel *lived* is more powerful than the Gospel *preached.*

6. We should "say so" before our loved ones in the home, before our fellow workers, and before all the world.

Daniel J. Curry

THE TESTIMONY OF THE REDEEMED

Psalm 107:2

I.   Let Us Ask, Who Are the Redeemed?

A. The word redeem means to buy back. It implies that some people who should have belonged to God, were dragged away, and now comes One and snatches them back. There are many expressions of this. Romans 7:14 says we were sold under sin, but Christ lifted the mortgage and set us free.

B. Galatians 3:13 says, "Christ hath redeemed us from the curse of the law, being made a curse for us." These and similar passages show the meaning of the word.

C. We were once lost, but we have been found. We were condemned, but we have been set free. We were moral wrecks, but He has salvaged us. We were children of the Devil, hell-bound; but Christ has saved us, changed us, and made us children of God, and set our feet in the path that leads to heaven. How great should be our gratitude!

II.   What Do the Redeemed Have to Say?

A. They have an experience to tell. Every redeemed one has a real experience, not just a theory, nor a fanciful idealism. As the man born blind when Christ healed him said, "I was blind, but now I see." He may not have been able to explain the processes, but he knew the fact. Paul never tired of telling his experience on the road to Damascus.

B. They have a gratitude to express. How can one recall the great blessing of salvation without being grateful? Are you ashamed of it? If a slave should be set free would he be grateful to his benefactor?

C. They have a recommendation to make. As one recommends a good physician to a sick friend, or as one recommends a given remedy to one in need, so let us recommend our Savior to the lost.

III.   Why Don't the Redeemed Say It?

A. They are commanded to tell it. He says we are witnesses, yet some do not bear witness.

B. Their silence fetters the church, and the cause of Christ.

C. There is much value and benefit in the testimony of the redeemed if they would faithfully tell it.

D. Some are ashamed to tell it because of the inconsistency of their lives. Some are timid, retiring and fearful, they need courage. God will help them if they will have it.

Sermons in the Making

LIVING PRAISE

The dead praise not the Lord, neither any that go down into silence. But we will bless the Lord from this time forth and for evermore. Praise the Lord (Ps. 115:17–18).

The living God should be adored by a living people. A blessing God should be blessed by a blessing people. Whatever others do, we ought to bless Jehovah. When we bless Him we should not rest until others do the same; we should cry to them, "Praise the Lord." Our example and our persuasion should rouse them to praise.

I. **A Mournful Memory.** "The dead praise not the Lord, neither any that go down into silence." This reminds us:

A. Of silenced voices in the choirs of Zion. Good people and true who neither sing nor speak among us any longer.

B. Of our own speedy silence. So far as this world is concerned we shall soon be among the dead and silent ones.

C. Of the ungodly around us, who are already spiritually dead and can no more praise the Lord than if they were mute.

II. **A Happy Resolution.** "But we will bless the Lord."

In the heart, song, testimony, actions, we are resolved to give the Lord our loving praise, because:

A. We are blessed of the Lord. Shall we not bless Him?

B. He will bless us. More and more will He reveal His love to us; let us praise Him more and more. Be this our steadfast vow, that we will bless the Lord come what may.

III. **An Appropriate Commencement.** "We will bless the Lord from this time forth."

A. When spiritually renewed and comforted. When the four times repeated words, "He will bless," have come true in our experience (vv. 12–14).

B. When led to confess Christ. Then should we begin the never-ending life-psalm. Service and song should go together.

C. When years end and begin—New Year's days, birthdays, etc.—let us bless God for:

Sins of the year forgiven.
Needs of the year supplied.
Mercies of the year enjoyed.

IV. **An Everlasting Continuance.** "From this time forth and for evermore."

A. Weariness shall not suspend it. We will renew our strength as we bless the Lord.

B. Final falling shall not end it. The Lord will keep our souls in His way and make us praise Him all our days.

C. Nor shall death so much as interrupt our songs, but raise them to a purer and fuller strain.

D. Nor shall any supposed calamity deprive the Lord of our gratitude. "The LORD gave, and the LORD hath taken away; blessed be the name of the LORD" (Job 1:21).

PRAISE IS THE highest function that any creature can discharge. The rabbis have a beautiful bit of teaching buried among their rubbish about angels. They say that there are two kinds of angels, the angels of service and the angels of praise, of which two orders the latter is the higher, and that no angel in it praises God twice; but having lifted up his voice in the psalm of heaven, then ceases to be. He has perfected his being, he has reached the height of his greatness, he has done what he was made for; let him fade away. The garb of legend is mean enough, but the thought it embodies is that ever true and solemn one, without which life is nothing: "Man's chief end is to glorify God."   —*Maclaren*

When we bless God for mercies we prolong them, and when we bless Him for miseries we usually end them. When we reach to praise, we have compassed the design of a dispensation and have reaped the harvest of it. Praise is a soul in flower, and a secret, hearty blessing of the Lord is the soul fruit-bearing. Praise is the honey of life, which a devout heart sucks from every bloom of providence and grace. As well be dead as be without praise; it is the crown of life.

Spurgeon